Overcoming Obstacles
and
Living Your Dreams

Overcoming Obstacles
and
Living Your Dreams

Carol Sligh

Illustrated by:
Jordan Sligh

authorHOUSE®

AuthorHouse™
1663 Liberty Drive
Bloomington, IN 47403
www.authorhouse.com
Phone: 1 (800) 839-8640

Published by AuthorHouse 10/13/2015

ISBN: 978-1-4389-2520-2 (sc)
ISBN: 978-1-5049-5352-8 (e)

Print information available on the last page.

Any people depicted in stock imagery provided by Thinkstock are models, and such images are being used for illustrative purposes only. Certain stock imagery © Thinkstock.

This book is printed on acid-free paper.

Table of Contents

Letter to Reader

Have you ever felt unable to make a decision or unable to figure out how to solve a problem? Have you ever wanted to accomplish so many things that you couldn't decide what to do first? Have you ever been so afraid to take the wrong step that you couldn't take any step at all? Have you recently felt overwhelmed, confused, or just "stuck"?

The reality is that everyone goes through feeling overwhelmed or "stuck" at some time or another. It's not a matter of intelligence, education, or professional achievements - we all encounter obstacles that are difficult to overcome but whether you will overcome your obstacles successfully or stay in a "stuck" place becomes **your decision**.

When you're feeling stuck, the way out can be as simple as deciding what to do first and then doing just that - taking one step at a time. However, some people try to avoid facing obstacles by pretending they don't exist or by blaming someone else. They bury their heads in the sand, hoping that they won't have to face reality and take action to solve the problem. They decide to do "nothing," or at least that's what they think they're doing - they don't realize that there is no *such thing as doing "nothing." A decision to do "nothing" is a decision itself - it's deciding* not *to solve the problem and choosing the consequences of allowing the problem to remain unresolved and possibly get worse. It's also choosing to allow the continuing negative impact of the problem on their family or other people in their life.*

Many people choose "the path of least resistance," doing whatever requires the least amount of effort or work on their part. Unfortunately, this is not always the best choice. You see, life always has consequences, and you can't avoid responsibility for solving a problem and its consequences simply by doing "nothing." Facing an obstacle and taking action to overcome it is always better than abdicating responsibility and then regretting it later.

> **"We must all suffer from one of two pains - the pain of discipline or the pain of regret. The difference is that discipline weighs ounces and regret weighs tons." - Jim Rohn**

Life is full of choices. We have to decide what options we will or won't accept. God shows us that we not only have choices, but that he loves us so much that he gives us the best option - he tells us to "choose life." When you choose life, you are choosing to receive the very best life God has to offer you physically, mentally, financially, and spiritually. You're making a decision to use the abilities that God gave you so that you can overcome adversity and embrace the future enthusiastically, knowing that you will accomplish your goals.

> **"I have set before you life and death, blessing and curses. Now choose life, so that you and your children may live." - Deuteronomy 30:29 NIV**

Your life is not determined by fate. There was a plan for your life that existed long before your parents were even born. You were given the talents and opportunities to carry out that plan, regardless of who your parents are or the environment in which you grew up.

Everyone is on earth for a purpose. Your purpose may be the solution to a significant problem, the answer to someone's prayers, or fulfillment of the needs of people who are depending on you to do what God intends you to do in their lives. God orders the steps that you take toward fulfilling your purpose in life, and you play a critical, active role in following those steps and ensuring that your destiny is fulfilled.

Throughout my life, I have learned through the experiences of others. From a young age, I realized that if I saw someone else get burned when they touched something, I didn't need to touch it myself to confirm that it was hot. Of course, I've also had to learn some things through my own experience, "the hard way," and I've made some mistakes that have caused me pain and heartache along the way. However, one of the most important lessons I've learned is to make the most of every opportunity and to learn as much as I can from others' mistakes and successes as well as my own experiences. Whether an experience is good or bad, there is always a lesson to be learned from it.

As you read this book, I hope that you will grow and learn from my experiences as well as from the people whose testimonies I will share with you. These experiences will also encourage you to pursue your dreams without fear or despite your fears. As you navigate through life's journeys, you can pursue your goals confidently and in accordance with God's plan while recognizing the signs that tell you when caution is needed. You can then adjust your course as needed and continue to proceed toward your destiny with God as your guide and inspiration and experience as your teacher.

The goals of this book are to:

- *Encourage you to acknowledge where you are in life right now and realize that you don't have to remain there.*
- *Identify seven obstacles that can prevent you from living your dreams and a life that is "full of purpose."*
- *Provide the necessary tools to assist you in overcoming obstacles in your life.*
- *Show you how to pursue your life goals and **fulfill your dreams**.*

This book will encourage, develop, and equip you to face and overcome the obstacles in your life. As you apply these principles, you will experience a transformation within yourself. Your perception about life and your ability to embrace it will change. You will view adversities in your life differently and use them as opportunities to grow.

WARNING: After reading this book and applying the tools provided, you will never be the same! As your coach and friend, I pray that you will have much success and receive all the blessings God has given you.

Enjoy!
Carol Sligh

How to Use This Book

This book addresses the seven most common obstacles to living a successful and fulfilled life. Each chapter identifies one of these obstacles and how to overcome it. Although it's most beneficial to read the book from the beginning through to the end, you may also start at the specific chapter that deals with what you believe to be your greatest obstacle. For each obstacle, an "Obstacle Buster" has also been provided. These can usually be applied immediately and may prove to be the critical keys to your success.

Like working with a coach, you can use this book to progress at the pace that is best for you. Everyone learns in stages and at different rates, and you may have some periods that are more difficult than others. Just continue to move at a pace that is comfortable for you. As long as you're moving forward, a small step is better than none at all.

As you complete the applications at the end of each chapter, answer as many of the questions as you can. If you can complete one exercise, that's great. If you can do more, that's even better.

I'd like to thank my dad, mom and all my family and friends for their support and encouragement, expecially Marjorie, Valerie and Euvonka who encouraged me during dark times.

I thank God, without whom this book would not have been possible.

I would also like to give a special thanks to my loving husband Mark and my smart and beautiful daughter Jordan...

Jordan, you have been an inspiration and an absolute joy. Thank you for working so diligently on the cover and showing that at 7 years old you can be an awesome illustrator.

Mark, I cherish you... my husband, lover, friend and teacher. I learn so much from you..... thank you.

Introduction

It was after a freak accident that my life changed. I had fallen and broken my hand and severely damaged the nerves in my upper-right arm. The injury was to my dominant hand, and the nerve damage produced a magnitude of pain that was unbearable. The doctor explained that there was no cure for "RSD" (reflex sympathetic dystrophy), but we could try different medications to reduce my pain. He felt that the pain cycle could possibly be broken with aggressive therapy, but it was too soon to determine how much permanent damage had occurred and whether I would be able to use my hand again at all. He added that if circulation and movement did not improve, the result could even be amputation.

Due to continuous pain, I found myself often crying. I spent many days lying in bed unable to get up. Although there was nothing physically wrong with my legs, I was spiritually and emotionally crippled. I felt helpless and started asking myself, "What's the use?" When I moved, I had pain; but even if I didn't move, I still hurt.

They say there are secret treasures in darkness, but I couldn't see any jewels in this experience. I found myself in one of the darkest places of my life. I couldn't cook, clean, or even take care of my personal needs, and the household chores continued to pile up. My world was crumbling. I began to lose all sense of hope...

Then one day in the midst of tears, I realized that this was not the kind of life that I was meant to live. I couldn't just "throw in the towel" and give up. I knew that there was a plan for my life and that I was meant to live a life filled with hope, good health, and success.

So I made a conscious decision to *overcome* my affliction. I decided that with faith and strong determination, I could create a new destiny for myself. It was time to get up, embrace life, and start living it to the fullest.

As soon as I decided to view my life differently, things began to get better. The treasures in my life started to unveil. I began to see the many blessings in and around me. Somehow I knew that a more fulfilled life was attainable, and that it was *up to me* to learn how to *overcome obstacles* and get the life I was meant to live.

We can all look back at our past and see how our experiences have helped us grow. My illness gave me a second chance to appreciate the little things that I had been taking for granted. Today I look at life from a different perspective and can truly say I am excited about each day and the opportunities that my future holds.

You too can learn to live a more meaningful and fulfilled life in which obstacles become opportunities to ensure your success. A fulfilled life is not just a privilege - it's a gift from God, and *you* can learn how to receive it.

Getting to the Root

The life you are living today has been shaped by the decisions you have made regarding your family, job, finances, and education. When you have made good decisions, you have enjoyed progress. When you have failed to identify and correct bad habits, such as poor financial management or lack of self-discipline, or you have missed opportunities to create a more positive environment, you may have become chained to an unpleasant life situation *by choice*.

You see, the problem or negative influence that you ignore or avoid doesn't just go away. You've merely buried it *alive*. It becomes a seed that you planted, and it is likely to grow. The fact that it may be temporarily hidden from view doesn't mean it no longer exists.

Eventually, a problem situation or behavior that has been buried will surface again.

Everything you do, everything you say, and everything you think is a **seed**, and for every seed you sow there will be a harvest. If you cut open a cantaloupe, you will see that it contains approximately 900 seeds. It took only one seed to produce 900 more. When you were conceived in the womb, it took only one fertilized egg cell to produce you; that single cell multiplied to produce the millions of cells that make up your unique human body. Famous inventions and large multimillion dollar companies started with a single thought, an idea, a plan - one *seed*.

Your basic beliefs and thought patterns produce the millions of decisions that you make throughout your life, resulting in the life that you create for yourself. Your life is a reflection of the choices you have made in the past, and each action you have taken was based on how you think. The thoughts that you have focused on have become the thinking patterns that guide your behavior and the results that you create on a daily basis. Your thoughts are the seeds that create the thinking patterns and belief systems that govern your entire life. These thought patterns can be the foundation for a successful lifestyle, or they can consume you if you don't take authority over them and create a foundation that will have a positive impact on your life.

Bringing About Change

Studies show that the average person has over 50,000 thoughts each day. We think about how to solve problems in our lives and whom to involve. We have opinions about people and places. The thousands of actions we take throughout the day are also based on our thoughts. Our individual thoughts create the thinking patterns that govern how we feel, how we approach challenges, and whether we will be successful in life.

In order to change your behavior, it is important that you remain in an aware, "conscious" state in which you can identify your thoughts and thinking patterns. If you tend to focus on negative things, you provide an environment in which negative seeds take root and attract more negative experiences into your life. If you tend to have positive thoughts, you will attract positive experiences. This is the Law of Attraction. The Law of Attraction means that what you *think* is what you *attract* to yourself, whether you want it or not. People who speak about and expect prosperity and a healthy life usually have it. People who constantly complain about illness and other misfortunes will usually have an unpleasant, unhealthy life. This is the Law of Attraction in action.

In fact, the first thing you focus on in the morning is likely to influence your entire day. Think about it. How many times have you awakened in the morning in a bad mood and then had a bad day? On days when you woke up happy, excited, and optimistic that something great would occur, has your day gone even better than expected? As soon as you wake up in the morning, it is important that you make a conscious choice to "Have a great day!" If you make up your mind that you will have a good day and you truly believe it, you will most likely have it. *What you focus on is what you will attract.*

In *The Game of Life*, Dawn Fields says that human beings are made up of body, mind, and spirit. Your mind houses the thoughts that are released by your beliefs, and your creative thoughts give you a "power" to imagine and therefore create success. For change to take place in your life it requires you to make a conscious decision to change and go against your daily regular behavior. The initial steps are to occur within your mind and resonate into your soul as a core belief and subsequently affect your behavior. All these transitions will bring about the desired results.

> *"If you do what you have always done;*
> *you'll get what you have always gotten." - Author Unknown*

Knee Deep in Squalor

The word "squalor" means to be marked by filth and degradation from neglect. This word describes the lives of many people who allow unaddressed issues to fester. Much of the chaos and disorganization in our lives is a result of neglecting the little things, such as the thoughts that we might think are insignificant because we don't understand the connection between our thoughts, thinking patterns, and actions.

> *"It is the little foxes that ruin the vineyards." - Solomon 2:15 (NIV amended)*

It is important to monitor and *direct your thought life* in a disciplined manner. Monitoring your thought life requires the self-discipline to be constantly aware of how you are thinking. Directing your thought life successfully requires choosing positive, constructive thoughts so that you can establish effective boundaries in your mind and life.

Research has proven that students who study on a regular, long-term basis usually do better overall than those who don't study in a timely manner and have to cram for the test the night before. The same principle applies to exercising. Exercising on a regular, frequent basis is much more beneficial than trying to get in shape by doing push-ups, sit-ups, or other exercises "once in a blue moon" or frantically the night before a special occasion. *Consistency, positive attitude,* and *self-discipline* are vital prerequisites for success.

When I was a child in grade school, I was instructed to memorize my multiplication tables. Every day, my teacher required each child to recite a set of tables in class. After memorizing the first five sets, I became somewhat bored. I began to daydream, and after a few consecutive days of not paying attention and not doing my homework, I began to fall behind in math. What I had considered to be so easy became too difficult for me to achieve even at a minimally satisfactory level. My failure to sow the correct seeds earlier also affected me later.

As a result of not memorizing my multiplication tables early on, it took me several years to learn how to solve simple mathematical and word problems. I struggled through each school year, hoping that once I had a new teacher and I was learning something new, it would get better; but it didn't. I hadn't learned the basics and grasped the fundamentals, so I was lost. I didn't understand that basic math also included the building blocks for algebra and geometry.

The problem became worse each year because I never asked for help. I was ashamed so it remained my little secret for much too long. I used the excuse that math was just "not my subject." So I continued to get bad grades in math, and I hated the subject more and more, never asking for help and never admitting that I didn't even know the basics.

It wasn't until my adult years that I finally acknowledged where I was and got help. I had to memorize my multiplication tables and get a tutor to help me catch up. To get good grades and be successful in this area, I also needed to sow seeds of self-discipline and focus. I wasn't dumb or stupid - I just needed to humble myself enough to be open to learning the fundamental formulas that are basic to mathematics, algebra, and word problems.

Change can improve any situation when you know where you are and where you want to go and you take action that may include getting the necessary help to get there. True lasting change takes place through basic knowledge and repetition of right decisions over a period of time. Taking those initial steps and exercising self-discipline along the way will promote positive change in your life.

If you haven't learned the basics for achieving success, including living a disciplined life, it's probably evident in several areas of your life. You may be one of those people who try to avoid taking responsibility for solving their problems, never accepting that most problems don't just go away. They will remain or appear again and again until you solve them. It may not be exactly the same manifestation of the problem the next time around, but problems will reappear in some form. You will have to repeat the lessons that you try to skip and the classes that you fail until you finally "get it."

As you thoughtfully and confidently address daily life situations, the lessons you learn from your experiences will prepare you for overcoming larger problems and obstacles later. If you don't exercise the resolve to overcome obstacles decisively, the lack of self-discipline will carry over into other areas of your life. Once you know and apply the basic formulas for success, you can build on them to learn more advanced formulas for addressing the more complicated and challenging situations in your life. Through this continuous learning process, you will be able to excel.

We can all make excuses. We are too busy, or we just don't have enough hours in the day, but we have to decide one thing - "Are you worth it?" You are your greatest asset. You can try to get through life by blaming others for your circumstances, but the results in your life have been brought about by the decisions that *you* have made. If you don't like what you see, you can change your thinking and your behavior to bring about more positive results.

> *"Life has a funny way of forcing you to go where you should have gone yourself."*
> *- Author Unknown*

Life has a "success formula," and overcoming obstacles requires **knowing** that there are alternative solutions, **choosing** the right approaches, and **addressing problems** with determination and a winning attitude. Never run from your problems - always face them directly. There is no better time than now to acknowledge the need to change and to take action to ensure that it occurs immediately.

<u>Summary</u>

Your behavior and actions are a direct result of your thought life. Lack of self-discipline in your thought life can hinder you in multiple areas of your life.

Everything you do, everything you say, everything you think is a "seed," and for every seed sown, a harvest will come forth. When you fail to identify and correct bad habits, such as poor financial management and lack of self-discipline, you may become chained to your problems and an unsatisfying life.

Life has a success formula, and to be successful, we must plant good seeds in our thought life and overcome obstacles in a constructive, timely, and confident manner.

OBSTACLE # 1:
You Don't Have A Specific Goal
And A Clear Plan To Attain It

If you've ever gone on a road trip, whether it was for a few hours or several days, you took certain steps toward your intended destination. You decided how to get there by either consciously outlining the route you would take, step by step, or by completing the steps of a familiar trip without having to think much about it. The steps you planned to take enabled you to arrive at your destination. Whether the route you took was based on conscious or subconscious decisions, you first had to identify your starting place. Then you had to figure out what steps to take to get to where you wanted to go.

One of the most frustrating experiences is driving to an unfamiliar destination without directions or a specific address. When you don't know exactly where you're going, especially if you haven't been there before, you may experience unnecessary frustration and anxiety. Not only is your travel time longer, but the trip also becomes very tedious.

For a short time in my life, I struggled with planning. I hadn't developed good habits in this area, so I didn't identify my goals or make plans for what I wanted to accomplish each day. Consequently, I never had enough time to complete all the tasks I wanted to complete. When I finally started to plan my time, I was able to accomplish more and be more productive each day and throughout my life.

With a plan and specific directions, your journey can be accomplished more smoothly, step by step. First, you must identify a specific goal and then focus on that goal as you develop and follow a "step-by-step" process on how to get there. Identifying your goals, planning your days, and keeping yourself on track will reduce unnecessary stress and ensure a more productive day through more constructive use of your time. It doesn't matter if you use the equivalent of a conventional map, a written plan, or an electronic tool like "MapQuest." You need to identify *where you are*, *where you want to end up,* and the *steps* you need to take to make necessary progress.

> *Obstacle Buster #1: To overcome an obstacle, it is important to identify a clear goal and specific steps to achieve it.*

How to Set and Achieve Your Goals

A successful plan starts with a clear goal and includes specific steps on how to achieve it. The goal must be simple, specific, realistic, and measurable. An example of a goal that doesn't meet these requirements is: "I want to improve my financial situation." A specific goal that does meet the requirements is: "I want to be free of all credit card debt and loans within five years."

Trying to live a successful, productive life without specific goals and plans is like looking for a job on a blank canvas or a deserted island. You wouldn't look for a job in an editorial column of a newspaper where there are no jobs listed and no employer names or contact information. You wouldn't expect to suddenly start receiving a regular paycheck by just wishing you had money or complaining about not having any. You probably wouldn't be successful at all. You need a specific goal and a plan for achieving it.

The plan for meeting a specific goal needs to be concise, straightforward, and practical. It should be based on an accurate assessment of your current situation and adequate information about how to get to where you want to be. This will require that you gain enough basic knowledge about the subject to formulate a realistic, step-by-step plan.

For example, if your goal is to be credit card debt free within five years (or whatever time period is reasonable for your situation), you need to include a complete assessment of all of your debts, including the amounts owed and monthly payments for each. What are the interest rates? Are these the best rates that you can get? Can you call and have your rates lowered or transfer your high-interest debts to lower interest cards or lenders? Check your spending habits, cut back on discretionary items, and apply that amount in addition to your regular payment to the smallest bill. You may need to prioritize your debts and pay them off one at a time, from the smaller to the larger amounts, or from the higher to the lower interest rates. When you have gathered all the necessary information you need, which may include consulting with an expert on the subject, you can devise a plan that is effective but realistic enough to ensure success.

When my husband Mark and I got married, we looked at our combined debts and realized that our total monthly minimum payments were more than our combined monthly income. We had virtually maxed out on our credit cards, and we felt as if we were working just to keep paying bills without ever making progress toward reducing our debt and achieving a better life.

As unpleasant as it was, we had to **acknowledge where we were** financially and decide to "do something about it." We soon identified a clear goal, developed a specific plan, and prayed about it. Then, of course, it was time to take action. We had to discipline ourselves to follow the plan. There were major adjustments required, but we knew that we could do it. Mark placed us on a budget and we cut up all of our credit cards. There is a simple saying that "if you don't like being in a hole, stop digging"; the quickest way for us to get out of debt was to stop using our credit cards.

Often people say they are *"believing"* God and praying for a change, but they fail to really make a commitment and the sacrifices required to get results. Mark and I had to stop "emotional spending," implement a budget, and minimize our spending. Every time we deviated from the budget, we had to acknowledge it and get back on course. After 4 1/2 years, we learned to manage our finances well, bringing us to zero balance in debt. All of our credit cards, vehicles, and loans were paid off.

Soon after our bills were under control, 9/11 occurred and Mark was laid off from his job with the airlines. The timing of the layoff was a blessing in disguise, because by this time our recurring bills were manageable. So Mark was able to take time off to go back to school, start a business, and pursue his purpose more directly. If we had not reduced our debt, we would have suffered tremendous financial hardship.

It took "discipline" and "consistency" to accomplish our goals. We had to continually evaluate and readjust our budget to accomplish the goal. Achieving your goals in life will take a plan and the self-discipline to follow it consistently. Mark and I are now able to set additional, higher goals towards financial independence. We took the necessary "natural" actions, including planning and taking the basic steps. We also prayed for direction and tithed, not as an option, but as part of our lifestyle.

Many people cringe at the idea of giving something away, especially money. They don't understand that money is not to be hoarded for our own self interests - it's a tool for contributing to society in accordance with God's purpose. Your tithing and giving are also seeds, and with every seed planted, there is the harvest to reap. Our basic needs - food, shelter, and clothing - are supposed to be met, but we are also responsible for sowing seeds in the lives of other people who need the blessings that God wants them to receive through us. We are just "vessels" to be used by God for his purposes, and we must allow and assist him in working through us.

Often what you think you need most is the very thing that you should start giving to others. It may be a few dollars, or it may start with giving your time. In fact, your time is worth more than money - it is more valuable than your material possessions because you only have one opportunity to use each available block of time. Once an hour passes, you can't get it back. You can save money and decide how to spend it later, but you can never store up time or relive the time you wasted yesterday.

Years ago, my husband and I began to understand the value of giving. Our lives changed when we began viewing ourselves as "givers" and acting accordingly. It is important to understand the benefits of giving and contributing to society by giving more of your time, talents, and encouragement as well as monetary support or tangible items that could make a big difference in the life of someone in need.

"Give and it shall be given to you."
- Luke 6:38 (NIV)

Where You Aim Is What You Will Hit

Maybe you have desires, but you're not clear on your goals or how to achieve them. A person can say, "I would like to go to school," but if they don't have a clear goal in mind, they might accumulate a large number of class credits but never receive the degree or certification that they need to get the job they want. If you don't know where you're going, how do you know which classes to take to get there?

Without a defined target, you may be participating in a "process" with no measurable "progress" because meaningful progress can only be measured based on how close you have come to achieving your goal. Clarity on your goal also facilitates advancement toward an achievement of that goal. It provides a basis for aligning your steps along the path that will lead more directly and efficiently to the goal.

"You cannot hit what you cannot see."
- Author Unknown

When you're mapping out the directions for reaching a particular destination, you focus on how to get there. Then when you're ready to go, you follow the route you mapped out, focusing on the process of driving, accelerating and slowing down as needed. You follow the traffic control signals, turn left or right along the way, and take the streets or freeways that you have chosen to take. You reach your destination by completing the actions that are appropriate for your starting place and where you want to go. As long as you plan and take the correct steps toward your destination, you will get the results you desire.

Several years ago, when the type of work I did required me to be prepared to use a firearm, I took a "refresher" shooting course to improve on my handgun-shooting techniques. In the first session, the instructor told me to shoot at a particular target several times. Then by looking at where the bullet round had hit on the target, he was able to explain to me exactly what I was doing incorrectly, based on the results that he had observed.

For the next two weeks, he retrained me to shoot my handgun with more accuracy. He explained that the problem was that I had been focusing on the target instead of aligning my "sights" (which are small metal protrusions located at the front and rear of the top of the gun). He told me to just focus my vision on "aligning the sights," which helped me to aim accurately by "lining up" the sights on the top of the weapon in a straight line before pulling the trigger. I didn't worry about stance, loading, or pulling the trigger until I mastered alignment, the immediate task at hand. It wasn't until later that he began to work with me on how to stand, breathe, and then pull the trigger.

As I put all the steps together, he reminded me that if I focused properly, I would get the best results. He explained that when I focus on the sights, everything outside of my line of focus should be blurred (creating an effect known as "tunnel vision," which for this exercise was desirable). Likewise, as you focus on taking the actions necessary to achieve your goal, everything else should be blurred. Everything else should be considered an unwanted distraction.

With the information given by my instructor, I focused clearly on my shooting sights, and when I slowly pulled the trigger, the bullet hit the 10 ring. Then I followed through by scanning the area, as would be necessary in a tactical situation to assess results and determine if there are any other threats. Then if no adjustments are necessary, it's appropriate to refocus on aligning the sights again. This is what is referred to as "follow through" or the "assessing" stage.

Once you have identified your goal and how to get there, you need to discipline yourself to focus on execution of the necessary steps for success. When executing the action plan, you can assess your progress to determine if any adjustment is needed in light of any significant changes to the environment. Then you can go back to following the action plan consistently until the ultimate goal is reached. In other words, ask yourself, "Is the plan working or are additional changes or adjustments necessary?" You can then refocus on your goal and continue executing the action steps again. **Your goals must be specific, measurable, and clear so that you are able to assess progress and evaluate what is working.**

Placing "Feet to Your Vision"

For every action, a reaction will occur, and for everything you do, there will be positive or negative consequences. This is the law of "cause and effect." Each time you take a series of steps and experience the reward of success, the process will be reinforced and will soon become second nature to you. As you initially focus on each step toward your life goals, the results may initially seem very distant or even impossible. Then as you continue your planned steps, practicing constructive thinking and self-discipline in executing the plan, the steps become easier and the goal becomes closer and clearer. This is what I refer to as placing your "feet to your vision."

> *"You are what you have always been; you'll be what you do now."*
> *- Author Unknown*

Most people focus on the results that they desire, but they don't do the proper legwork to get there, so they don't end up where they want to be. If you have a clear goal that can easily be seen and measured, and you're consistent in doing what's necessary to achieve that goal, it will be met. To be a lifelong "career student" is fine for some people, but it is much more beneficial to not only *gain* knowledge but also *do* something with it. They say knowledge is power, but that's not necessarily true - it's how you *use* knowledge that determines how powerful it can be.

In Proverbs 4:5, it states, "Let your eyes look straight ahead, fix your gaze directly before you." In shooting my handgun, it was important for me to focus on the sights and not the target or anything around me. In pursuing your goal, it is important that you not become distracted with things around you. When you're distracted from your original focus or interest, your success can be jeopardized. If you find yourself frequently distracted, you must refocus on your goal and the steps that will ensure your achievement of that goal, or may never complete your goals successfully.

You may have heard the saying "Jack of all trades, master of none." Although multi-tasking is a valuable skill, it is not always the best way of accomplishing one's life goals. It's admirable to be able to perform various tasks, but if you are unable to focus on the highest-priority task at hand, you may not be productive in some situations. This can make you ineffective in pursuing your ultimate goal. You can complete numerous tasks at once, but you may not be as accurate and successful as when you are doing one thing at a time in the proper sequence. The more tasks you are juggling, the less capable you are of mastering a particular area, and important steps or priorities may fall by the wayside.

It is important to not only write plans down, but also to make them clear and concise.

> *"Come you who are blessed by my Father; take your inheritance, the Kingdom prepared you since the creation of the world."*
> *Matthew 25:34 (NIV)*

This verse specifies actions that are required of you, even though everything is prepared for your involvement. You have to "come" and also "take" what is rightfully yours. When you take action, it is important to "place feet to your vision" rather than always expecting someone else to do the "heavy lifting."

Imagine that a banker calls you and says, "Hello, sir/ma'am. Your name has been randomly selected to pay off your mortgage free and clear. We will give you the cash. This is a promotion, no strings attached. All you need to do is to come down to the office and receive your check." What would you do? Would you take the necessary steps to get to the bank?

If your answer is yes, then why treat your dreams any differently? There are always steps that you can take immediately to get closer to accomplishing your dreams.

Taking action and planning

What can you recall ever starting and completing successfully? It can be something as simple as successfully transferring from one grade or level of school/college to another, or applying for a specific job or promotion. What steps did it require? For instance, to complete a course your teacher gave you a syllabus with all the requirements. The teacher also implemented a plan that you had to follow with scheduled tests and required points that culminated in the following class.

- List five things you would like to change in your life. *Note: All goals should be specific, measurable, attainable, and realistic.* Choose to accomplish three of the smallest goals (short term).
- Why do you want to accomplish this goal? Are you passionate about it? Is it important to you? Remember that it is important that your goals are important to *YOU.* You are the driver. There are times you have to encourage yourself especially when others aren't encouraging. Write down how your life would be different once you accomplished this goal.

- What do you need to do accomplish this goal? For instance, let's say it is voiceovers. You want to someday do that for a living. It sounds interesting, but you have no idea *how* to even begin. Your short-term goal is not becoming a world-renowned voiceover professional in the industry. It is becoming *knowledgeable* and *familiar* with that particular industry. How much does it pay? Are there schools or classes you can take? (Remember that the wonderful world of the Internet is a great resource for you.)

- Write down who you know personally or who you have heard of that is doing voiceovers. If you know them call them personally and invite them for coffee or lunch on your dime. Let them know that you've heard they do this work or you admire their work. (*BE HONEST.*) If they are truly confident in what they do, they will be open and not intimidated. If they refuse, politely thank them for their time and do not take it personally. Your gift will make room for you, and there are others waiting to connect with you to accomplish a portion of their path in helping you. No one ever became successful without the help of others. Take notes at your meeting and listen…listen and then ask questions. Your meetings can be either in person or by telephone to make it convenient for the person. Make a folder for your notes and research done and ask for suggestions about how you can get started and then attempt the suggestions. Also ask them if it is alright to follow up with the outcome. Most people will be impressed that you took their advice and assist you with any roadblocks you encounter. (Never take it personally if a person declines from assisting you. For every "no" received you are one step closer to the odds of receiving a "yes".)

Sowing in Good Soil

So far we have discussed the importance of identifying clear goals, developing a specific plan, and having the resolve to stick to the plan while taking authority over negative thoughts and distractions that may impede your progress. These are all basic steps that are necessary for overcoming obstacles and enjoying a fulfilling life. These actions represent the seeds that you must sow to reap the harvest that you can count on if you sow in good soil. Sowing in good soil requires that you maintain a pure heart, walk in love, resist distractions, and observe the other basic principles for enjoying a fulfilled life. You might have a clear goal and a solid plan in one area of your life, but if you constantly have revenge or wrong motives in your heart in another area, you can't expect to be rewarded with overall success.

Yeast is a very strong ingredient. Imagine that I have a package of yeast, maybe a handful. If I pour it onto the ground, nothing will happen. But if I take the same yeast, place it into a bowl, and add flour and water, then something happens. The yeast enables the dough to rise, and when baked, it makes bread.

Like with the dough mixture, if you use the right ingredients and take the correct steps in your life, *you also can rise.* Your daily decisions guide your steps and shape the path that takes you through the life you are living. The clearer you are about where you are going, the easier it will be to get there.

If someone decided to drop out of school and rob a bank, these choices would tremendously impact the person's life for many years and in many ways. Someone who chooses to further their education, improve their job performance, or pursue a particular new field can positively improve their lifestyle and the lifestyle of their family. By making wise decisions and thereby choosing a better, more positive lifestyle, you will also be able to contribute to a higher purpose and help others to achieve their purpose as well.

I personally encourage everyone to continue to learn daily. However, having a college degree is not everything. Even with a college degree, you are not guaranteed success or complete fulfillment in life. A degree, like money, is not an ultimate purpose but merely a tool. Furthermore, you can have all the degrees and riches you desire but still lose your life if your heart and your motives are not in alignment with the Word of God. Whatever you accomplish in life, having the right heart and motives will give you more leverage to receive prosperity in your life so that you can in turn help others.

Olga, my friend Jon's wife, is an example of the importance of having the correct motives and continually sowing good seeds in your life. An immigrant from Mexico, Olga had the courage to leave her home and a life of poverty to come to this country. Once she arrived here, Olga began working through a temporary agency doing clerical work for a large, successful company. When she was released from the company at the end of her assignment, she told her husband how much she enjoyed the job and how disappointed she was about having to leave. Her husband then asked her a question that changed her life. He asked, "Are you passionate about your job?" When she emphatically replied, "Yes," he told her to tell them that she would work for free.

So during the day Olga volunteered for this company and at night she took computer classes. Her coworkers frequently laughed at her and told her how silly it was to work for free, but that was the farthest thing from the truth. Olga was gaining experience, learning more each day, and planting seeds of goodness that would eventually pay off.

Managers were so impressed with Olga's work that she was eventually rehired as a clerical assistant. Then she became the manager of the Payroll Department. She is now responsible for processing over 200 employees' paychecks. She is just as conscientious now as she was 10 years ago. Olga doesn't have a college degree, but she does have the corner office supervising others. Nothing stopped her from achieving her dream, because she had a high degree of passion, a good heart, and the right motives.

Regardless of your situation, you can always sow good seeds by practicing strong faith and helping someone else. What you give someone can be as simple as a smile, a few encouraging words, or your time. Remember that every decision you make and everything you do is a seed, and for every seed there is a harvest that reflects the nature of the seed that was sown, the soil it was into, and the manner in which it was cultivated.

How Your Past Experiences Develop Your Character

There are things that happen in your life that may seem to be a mistake or a bad hand dealt to you. As time goes on, however, you will begin to see how everything that has occurred in your life, whether good or bad, was for a good purpose. When you sow good seeds, both positive and negative experiences fall into place for God's greater plan. Your positive experiences are the rewards that reinforce the good decisions you have made, and the negative experiences develop your character so that you have the wisdom and fortitude to recognize and overcome obstacles more effectively each time you encounter them later.

Several years ago, I was assigned by management to work with a fellow employee to complete a major project. I did almost all of the work, but upon completion of the project, my coworker took all the credit and ended up being promoted. At first, I was very bitter, angry, and humiliated, but soon I realized that being angry was not productive and not healthy.

The change in my attitude turned out to be a blessing. Someone else in management saw the project, was very impressed, and knew that I had been responsible for its success. I was then chosen to represent the organization in a high-profile position that I would have been ineligible for if I had received the promotion. The job that I did accept allowed me to grow and opened many doors to new contacts and additional positions. Sometimes in life unpleasant situations that challenge us are placed in our lives for a reason - not to devastate us, but to provide unique opportunities to *develop our character.*

Your development is a gradual process. It doesn't happen overnight. Even if on the surface you are experiencing something that seems terrible, look at life as your teacher and your experiences as the tests that help to reinforce what you have learned or identify the areas in which you need to develop further. Keep in mind that "life has a funny way of pushing you to a place where you should have gone by yourself."

In Romans 5:3-5 the apostle Paul says, "We also rejoice in our sufferings, because we know that suffering produces perseverance, perseverance [produces] character and character hope, and hope does not disappoint us because God has poured out his love into our hearts by the Holy Spirit whom he has given us." Paul was encouraging us to get excited when we're faced with obstacles, because in the midst of adversity, we develop strength.

> **"Consider it pure joy, my brothers, whenever you face trials of many kinds."**
> **- James 1:2 (NIV)**

This verse includes two key words - "consider" and "many." To "consider" is to think carefully, to take into account, or to treat an attentive or kind way. When you are facing adversity, you are not expected to deny what you are going through but to maintain a positive outlook through all of life's hurdles. These hurdles are opportunities to learn and to change or broaden your perspective.

It is inevitable that adversity will occur and that there will be multiple trials. When you face a difficult situation, you may not be able to change it directly, but you can change *how you choose to react* to it. The apostle Paul said that we should "consider it pure joy" *whenever* we face trials. When faced with adversity, it is important that you maintain a consistently positive, constructive attitude to *"overcome"* obstacles in each situation that occurs. You never want to deny your pain, misfortunes, or tragedies, but keep in mind that difficulties in life can build your character in ways that you could never achieve with only positive experiences.

As you overcome adversity, your trust in God increases. You begin to experience things in your life that strengthen your faith. These experiences become milestones along the journey of life and tools for you to use as you move forward. Today, you may look back on previous challenges that seemed impossible to handle at the time and now you realize how you were able to overcome them rather than letting them overcome you.

> **"Your past experiences develop your character."**
> **- Author Unknown**

As you encounter each test in life, keep in mind that all things, including trials and tribulations, come to an end. There is a season for everything. After every winter comes the spring, summer, and fall. Each season in your life plays a specific role in building on your unique set of experiences and developing your character.

I recall times in my life when I wished I could change something that occurred in my past. I found myself reliving the experience in my mind, but regardless of my desire to "change" my past, I soon realized that it was virtually impossible. You can't change the past, but it is important to use your experiences and the wisdom to make the future better, regardless of the past. Your past experiences can improve your future decisions.

Things that were unpleasant in your life may have caused you pain or to second-guess the way you reacted. Often, negative scenarios replay in your head and become more and more unpleasant. Every time you allow yourself to relive these situations, you are feeding that negative thought and its impact on your thinking grows. Negative emotions may begin to take over and self-condemnation and regret begin to occur, controlling your present decisions and ultimately your future. As you replay the past in your head, you tend to relive the most negative aspects of those experiences.

Try it now. Take a moment to think of a terrible past experience that really angered you, upset you, or made you afraid...

As you recall what happened and how it made you feel, is your facial expression changing? What about your heart rate or breathing? Did your muscles tighten, even though the incident occurred some time ago, or when you were just a child? Even today, you might feel similar to how you felt as that little child, perhaps vulnerable or afraid, even though the original incident occurred many years ago.

Instead of reliving negative experiences from the past, recall the positive memories so that you can reinforce the actions, feelings, and positive expectations associated with them. This is a good way to develop positive expectations and the good habits that lead to success in life.

Now think of something that happened to you that was wonderful. Maybe you received some exciting news or accomplished an important goal. Or you can imagine that you received $1 million, no strings attached, a dream house, a child, or whatever excites you and has you leaping for joy. As you recall or imagine this experience, how do you feel? Are you happy? Are you smiling? Is your positive outlook likely to attract people who are loving and supportive?

Once again, your thoughts are very powerful in determining how you feel and how you react today, even if those thoughts are about imaginary scenarios or recollections from the past. If you choose to relive negative scenarios over and over again, they can cause you to question yourself. Brooding about losses or other negative experiences can stifle you and keep you living in the past, dwelling on what you used to do or used to have. Though it can be beneficial to reflect for the purpose of learning or appreciating how you overcame a negative situation, don't become obsessed with your past, because it hinders your ability to embrace the future in a positive, productive way.

No Progress Without a Process

When you're doing the laundry, you put your clothes into the washing machine dirty and they come out clean. Your clothes went through a process in order to become clean, and the result was evidence of progress. A woman's menstrual cycle is also an example of progress through a process. It is the "process" that prepares the uterus for possible embedding of a fertilized egg and the development of a new human being. Even "Mother Nature" has a "process" to achieve progress.

When burn victims are treated for serious burns on their bodies, there is a process of scraping the skin to remove the damaged layer and allow the healing process to take place as the cells regenerate. This process of scraping the skin can be done several times to promote healing, even though it will be painful. In life, you will also undergo cycles or a "process" while you develop. There will be ups and downs throughout your life, and both positive and negative experiences have their place.

Your Misery Can Become Your Ministry

Your misery can become your ministry and a vehicle to help others. Something terrible in your life can be used to help others. Some of the best drug-abuse counselors are previous abusers. They are familiar with all the manipulation tactics and lies because they have "been there" themselves. Previous miseries can provide you with a platform to contribute to society and bring about a change. William Griffith Wilson (Bill W.) overcame alcoholism and founded the 12-step program that has helped millions of people. What better way to contribute to society than in an area in which you are passionate and driven for a cause you lived and experienced?

You can also be so infuriated by something that it compels you to want to change it. Look at people such as Erin Brockovich, Martin Luther King Jr., and Nelson Mandela. These people were driven by an inner spirit, passion, and drive that are inexplicable to other people who would have just given up. These people went beyond themselves in order to benefit others.

Erin Brockovich was a woman who had a car accident that was not her fault. Her attorneys failed to obtain a settlement of a lawsuit filed. Due to financial constraints, Erin then begged her attorney, Ed Masry, to hire her. While employed by her attorney, Erin soon stumbled onto a cover-up involving contaminated water in a local community. Concerned and as a voice for the victims who were gravely ill or dying, Erin and Ed engaged the help of a large law firm and went on to negotiate the largest settlement ever paid in a direct action lawsuit in U.S. history - $333 million.

What angers or infuriates you can be a clue to your purpose in life. Your hurts and pains can become a catapult for you and an inspiration for others. Your passion or rage can motivate you to embark on a mission to help bring about change. For example, it was the brutal 1994 rape and murder of seven-year-old Megan Kanka that prompted the public demand for broad-based community notification. Washington State's 1990 Community Protection Act included America's first law authorizing public notifications when dangerous sex offenders are released into the community. On May 17, 1996, President Clinton signed Megan's Law, which requires the registration of sex offenders and notification to the community. This change took place because of a tragic incident that infuriated others. No one wanted this tragedy to occur, but the public's response to the loss of Megan Kanka's life has saved the lives of many other children. A similar incident occurred when Polly Klaas, a 12-year-old girl, was abducted from her bedroom and brutally murdered. We now have several nonprofit foundations such as the Polly Klaas Foundation to educate parents regarding child abduction. This incident motivated people to take action for a cause that was very worthwhile and fulfilled their purpose in life.

Ordinary people can accomplish goals that may have appeared to be unattainable. They can effect change when they are empowered by their inner spirit and they refuse to allow anything or anyone to stop them. It may be a schoolteacher, police officer, pastor, doctor, or nurse with a particular passion and goals. They each contribute to society as they reach out to help others. They may impact the individuals whose lives they touch by teaching them a skill, imparting knowledge, or providing inspiration or encouragement to others. You too have received something from everyone who has touched your life.

> *"Before I formed you in the womb I knew you; before you were born, I set you apart." - Jeremiah 1:4 (NIV)*

The above quote is one of my favorites. It means that no matter what happens to you in life, it is possible to live your dreams because you have a purpose that supersedes any obstacles that you may face. God is able to use anyone. You can accomplish your goals and live your dreams, not in your own strength, but by allowing the Holy Spirit to work through you. Just ask and believe, and you will receive.

> *"Now unto him who is able to do exceedingly and abundantly above all that you could ask or think, according to the power that dwells within you." - Ephesians 3:20 (KJV)*

You can use the worst experiences of your life to develop wisdom and character and to help others through a process of reciprocal benefit. A few years ago, a previous drug user who was enrolled in a drug-abuse counseling course began to share with the class all the terrible things she had done to get her next "fix." She said that if there was a name for it, she had done it, everything except murder. Even after she had served her sentence, she still suffered further consequences. "With two felonies on my record," she explained, "there were no jobs I could get, except helping others [to overcome] what I had previously struggled with for years." So she did just that. She began helping others through the recovery process and she was able to "give back" what she had "stolen from society." Her misery became her ministry.

You Are Not a Mistake

There was a reason why you were born. You were born with the unique abilities that you have. You encounter specific people in your life for a purpose. You and your talents are not a mistake. The obstacles that occur in your life are not mistakes and not a surprise to God. God has given you exactly what you need to fulfill your purpose and have an enjoyable, fulfilled life.

There are many successful and famous people who grew up with learning disabilities. These include Olympic diver Greg Louganis, financial executive Charles Schwab, and actor Danny Glover. Even if you have or believe that you have a disability, you can overcome it and use it to fulfill your purpose for your life. Most people are not aware that Danny Glover suffers from dyslexia. Despite this, he has used his success and celebrity status to advance many community programs and worthy causes, such as AIDS awareness in South Africa and the advancement of minority youth. He once stated, "Had I not been dyslexic, I might have chosen a different profession. Acting gave me a way of expressing some of the inner life that was raging inside of me as a result of my dyslexia." During your life, you too will have experiences that cause difficulty and discomfort, but if you refuse to give up, it will all work out for your good.

A pearl is very beautiful, but it was not always this way. It started out as a grain of sand that was an irritation to the oyster, a foreign object within the shell. The grain of sand undergoes a process that results in a beautiful pearl. The same is also true with a diamond. Prior to undergoing a process, it resembled a dark piece of coal. This piece of carbon becomes a diamond after purification through fire. Both of these items underwent a process that transformed it. Likewise, everything you experience in life occurs for a purpose.

> *"All things work together for good of those who love God, to those who are the called according to His purpose." - Romans 8:28 (NKJV)*

A good friend of mine, Sergio, decided to join his department's softball team. The local fire department soon challenged them to a match. Sergio and his team members practiced consistently three times a week in preparation for the big day. On the day of the event, he was excited and ready to play, but two department supervisors who had not attended any practices showed up and demanded to participate. In order to accommodate them, Sergio and another employee were benched for almost the entire game.

Angered by what had occurred, Sergio decided to start his own team. He was determined that no one on the team he started would ever have to go through the humiliation and disappointment he had experienced. He recruited friends and relatives employed by local city departments. His new team became very good, made it to the playoffs twice, and won numerous trophies. It has been a very rewarding experience for Sergio and all of his team members. They would not have existed had it not been for Sergio's resolve to do something good as a result of a bad experience.

Many mishaps, mistakes, or injustices will happen on the job, in your everyday life, or in your family. As you learn and develop, these experiences can become springboards for you and can help others. You may be unable to see the purpose of an experience while it is occurring, but you can be sure that it is part of a greater plan.

Nothing just happens. If you chose this book in search of answers or direction on your journey, expect the previously impossible to become possible. You are the driver to your destiny. You are able to determine *your* destination. Expect change - your life will never be the same. If this book was a gift, consider it a seed that will produce a good harvest in you. A seed may appear small, but that same seed can become a forest or vineyard. A seed in the right soil will always produce something larger. The fact that this book is in your hands is no coincidence - we met by an ordained appointment.

Summary

- If you have a desire to reach a specific goal, there has to be a *step-by-step process* for how to get there.
- As you focus on the action steps of your goals, the results will come.
- There is always something you can do to get closer to your dreams.
- Your development is a gradual process.
- You never want to deny any pain, misfortune, or tragedy that you may experience, but life's difficulties can truly build your character.
- There is a season for everything. After every winter there is a spring, and after every summer there is a fall. Each season in your life is important and plays a specific role.

- The worst things that have happened in your life can be used to help others and become a platform for you to pursue your purpose and your dreams.

Application

1. What problems in your life are you avoiding rather than addressing in a timely manner? Has avoidance resulted in the problem expanding over a period of time?
2. What decisions and/or actions would bring about a more desirable result? Would it help to delegate, schedule time aside to focus on it, remove or prioritize it with your daily work schedule?
3. List five things that you have avoided doing. Which tasks can you delegate to someone else? Put in writing a plan to address one task that you can commit to completing in a realistic time period.

Example: I don't like "housework," but I love a clean house. I used to put off vacuuming and dusting, and I would get frustrated. So my husband and I agreed that because of our busy schedules, it would be easier to "delegate" cleaning to a maid service. So we hired one. That decision eliminated some of our stress, and we only had to maintain cleaning between her scheduled visits.

OBSTACLE #2:
You're Unable To See Yourself Attaining Your Goal

Every human being is unique. No two people were created the same. We are all special. Even identical twins do not have the same fingerprints - each of us was given our own. God has a unique purpose and a special plan for each of us.

> *"I am God, and there is none like me. I make known the end from the beginning...*
> *My purpose will stand and I will do all that I please. - Isaiah 46:9 (NIV amended)*

Before the beginning was the end. The way that God worked backwards was ingenious. According to his plan, no matter what decisions we make in life, we will have sufficient opportunities to end up where he needs us to be. Of course, he gave us free will and an opportunity to receive the life he has planned for us. All you have to do is to receive it. Your chances for success are not based on who you are or where you have been. He freely gives all of us what we need because he loves us. He continually directs our paths so that we can be successful and his will can be accomplished.

The life you are living is the direct result of decisions you made or chose not to make. Your success is more than "destiny." It is the "determination" to strive for higher altitudes while refusing to just accept whatever life dishes out to you. It is an inner drive and a flame that can be quenched by contributing to society and others, but not by mere material gain.

Debbi was a young housewife with no business experience. At the age of 20, she had a dream, a recipe, and a passion for sharing her chocolate chip cookies. She managed to do what most people considered impossible. Debbi convinced a bank to finance her business concept, which had never been proven and was not likely to be successful. This was in 1977.

Baker, founder, and former chairman of Mrs. Fields Cookies, Debbi Fields ended up acquiring 25 years of entrepreneurial, operational, and managerial experience, all of it earned in a company she built literally from scratch. Mrs. Fields has since sold the company for $450 million. Mrs. Fields Cookies is still a market leader among fresh-baked cookie stores.

Obstacle Buster # 2: Believe that you can achieve your goals.

Each of us has the capability of contributing to society through our gifts and talents. It is through these gifts that we can seek to inspire others and leave a legacy to continue on.

Everyone has a gift. Some people are well aware of their abilities, and others feel they have no special talents at all. Your gifts, however, are not for you but for others. We are blessed to be a blessing. God helps us so that he can work through us for others.

"Each one should use whatever gift he has received to serve others."
- 1 Peter 4:10 (NIV)

Regardless of whether you can imagine yourself accomplishing more, the Holy Spirit dwells within and can take over if you allow him to. Fulfilling your dreams is possible, regardless of your past. You are able to do "exceedingly" (more than) and "abundantly" (amply supplied) more than you could ever do by yourself.

Not everyone allows the Holy Spirit to work through them, but God can use anyone at any time for his purpose. If you are willing to allow it, God is able to guide and direct you to live the life he planned for you. To help you with this, you can pray the following prayer:

> *Dear Heavenly Father;*
>
> *I believe you died for my sins, and I accept you as my personal savior. I ask you to rule and reign in my life. I submit to you and want to be all you plan for my life. Lead me, guide me, and teach me your ways, not mine, in Jesus's name.*
>
> *Amen.*

God is serious about accomplishing his purpose throughout the earth, regardless of where you were born or whatever obstacles or disability you may think you have. God not only has a plan for your life, but he is still in control. Living a life of purpose is fulfilling and rewarding. It replaces the void you may sometimes feel within.

> **"In his heart, a man plans his course, but the Lord determines his steps."**
> **- Proverbs 16:9 (NIV)**

The Choice Is Yours

When I gave my life completely to God, I asked him for a life that reflected more of his will and less of my own, so that he could use me more. At first it was easy. I prayed and heard God's voice and good things happened. I could see that God was clearly moving in my life. But then it seemed that he was becoming more distant. I began to feel empty inside and became frustrated and disheartened. I continue to seek him more earnestly, and much more effort was required before I finally felt more connected with him again.

God's thoughts toward us are of good and not evil. Depression is the "lack of expression," and anything lacking is not from God. He allows us to have unpleasant experiences as opportunities to grow. God rewards those who seek him, and what we seek is what we will eventually find. The Lord wanted to develop me. It was time for me to grow and trust him. As I continued to read his word, I was increasing and building my spiritual life, thus filling the void within.

A child learns to walk one step at a time, through trial and error. At first, the parent may hold the child's hands as he practices moving one foot forward at a time. As a child takes his first steps while balancing himself alone, the parent may encourage the child to take a few more steps by stepping further away with their hands stretched out toward the child. As the child begins to develop more skill and confidence, the parent allows a child to take more and more steps towards them. Throughout life, God is always there with arms open to help us through the learning process. You just have to take the steps towards your Heavenly Father and trust that he will be there for you with open arms.

"The plans of the Lord stand firm forever."
Psalms 33:10-11 (NIV)

There are no mistakes too bad or too big for God. You will always be usable to God. Continue to move forward, no matter how many times you stumble and fall.

One of the keys to achieving your goals is to *believe* you can do it. Allow yourself to dream, search within yourself, and seek God as to what his plan and will is for your life. You've probably heard the saying "As a man thinks in his heart, so is he." About 95 percent of our decisions and actions are determined by our subconscious. The subconscious houses our core beliefs that may be permanently engrained in our minds. What you practice becomes second nature. You do it "without thinking about it" because it is now habitual.

> **"Many are the plans in a man's heart, but it is the Lord's purpose that prevails." - Proverbs 17-21 (NIV)**

Young police recruits in the police academy are taught techniques over and over again. As they repeat these shooting and self-defense techniques, it becomes second nature for them. In fact, when graduates are faced with real-life situations, studies have shown that they will revert to what they were taught and what they practiced. In a moment of fear or pressure, you will do what you have practiced without thinking about it. What you practice is what you will do. If you don't learn what to do or you don't practice, you will do "nothing" when you encounter difficulties.

One of the quickest ways to change your beliefs is through visualization and positive self-talk. If you can mentally or visually see it, you can achieve it. I have a friend named Chuck who is almost 50 years old but is a competitive runner who maintains his physical fitness. As part of his training, he visualizes himself crossing the finish line and winning the race. He has won numerous medals and is faster than most runners in younger age categories. He explained that as part of his program he sees himself at the location where he will participate successfully. In his mind, he can hear the crowd, and he feels the joy of winning on a daily basis. He trains not only his body but also his *mind*. Chuck believes that winning is "normal" - he believes that he is supposed to win. Whatever you believe is "normal" becomes your reality and your natural response.

Childbirth labor is one of the most excruciating pains a woman can ever endure. A mother's good manners and characteristic demeanor can completely change during contractions. Most women still choose to have babies anyway. Painful contractions during delivery are considered a "normal" part of the birthing experience. Many women will talk about the pregnancy and the pain, but their main focus is the final result - the baby, the gift of a child. Whatever you believe to be "normal" will be acceptable and will dominate your life.

If a child is told by people around him that "you're stupid" or "you're never going to amount to anything," after a while the child believes it, especially if he heard it from family, peers, or those whom he trusts and looks up to. He is likely to internalize these lies and develop very low self-expectations. As an adult, he may find himself struggling, and bad things may keep happening in his life. If he believes this is normal, this mindset and behavior can become prevalent in his life. Society and the people you associate with can directly impact your thoughts, beliefs, and the life you are living.

Our subconscious is the hard drive of our brain. It is a storage place of past disappointments, experiences, and beliefs. The subconscious stores information that is passed down from our family, friends, and society. If you believe that you will never be successful, you'll sabotage yourself and always end up with the same undesirable results. By looking at your goals and assessing your accomplishments, both positive and negative, you can identify where you are and what you need to change in order to accomplish your goals. Through visualization, you can prepare yourself for success and for overcoming obstacles with ease. As you focus on success, what you visualize occurs through the Law of Attraction.

Visualize Your Success

By visualizing achievement of your desired goal, you are programming your mind to accept that "this is normal." Visualization can be improved by practicing the following exercises:

1. Imagine yourself meeting your goals and how success feels.
2. Put your goals in writing and set a deadline date. Write a letter.

3. Complete a vision board. Use visual arts such as pictures, brochures, and reminders of what you aspire to attain. Place it on walls where you will see it several times a day.

Summary

- Living a life of purpose is rewarding and fulfilling and replaces the void that you may sometimes feel within.
- Believe that you will achieve your goals.
- When you become overwhelmed by fear or pressure, you will do what you have practiced doing without thinking about it. If you have developed a habit of allowing your problems to dominate your life rather than taking authority for overcoming obstacles, that is what you will continue to do until you make up your mind to take charge and develop a new pattern of thinking and behavior.

Application

1. Ask yourself, "What is my intention for the future? What do I want to happen? What will move me closer to my goal?" Put your answers in writing.
2. Visualize what you want to have already accomplished and continue to visualize it.
3. Illustrate your desire with pictures. Collect or create visual images of your goal.
4. Dedicate at least 30 minutes of every day to investing in your dream, whether it is a phone call, research, or scheduling time to attend a class. Invest in yourself daily. "Place feet to your dream." (We will speak further on this subject in the final chapter.)

OBSTACLE #3:
Getting Stuck In Your "Comfort Zone"

The "comfort zone" can literally kill you. After a while, stagnant water can become toxic and poisonous. Remaining in the "comfort zone" can be deadly. It slowly kills your vision and hemorrhages your dream.

One day while walking through my backyard, I noticed a stack of logs and bricks and a broken cement fountain that had been there against the garage for two or three years. Prior to this, our gardener had cut down one of our trees that had pretty much died.

When he asked if we wanted to keep the lumber and bricks that had been around the tree, I agreed, even though I didn't have a fireplace to burn the logs. I planned to take the logs to my mother-in-law, who did have a fireplace to use them.

But the lumber never made it to my in-laws, and I never replaced the tree, so I didn't use the bricks or the fountain. The rubble became an eyesore. Although it was in a neat pile at the side of the garage, it was still out of place, so after several years, I decided to throw it all away. As I picked up the final logs that were lying on the ground, a bunch of bugs and worms that were under it began to scurry. The logs had been there so long that the slugs had made a home under it.

Obstacle Buster #3: Get out of your comfort zone and practice pushing through to build a new level of strength.

The things we don't take care of can be a breeding ground for bad habits and chaos. It may look okay on the surface, but if you dig deep enough, you may find something not so appealing. When someone goes to the dermatologist (a doctor specializing in the skin), the doctor gives her medication and advises her to use a particular ointment. He tells her that the condition may appear to become worse before it looks better, but she should just keep applying it until her acne clears up (unless, of course, an allergic reaction occurs). At first the condition may look worse because in addition to treating the surface of the skin, the medication is also pulling out impurities from beneath the surface. The patient just has to trust that if she continues using the medicine consistently, she will eventually see improvement.

As you move forward in life in any particular direction, anticipate that you will feel some discomfort. It is through this discomfort that we have an opportunity to grow. For example, when we are exercising, stretching is important for flexibility and critical for massive, rapid muscle growth. Stretching not only minimizes injuries, but it also helps increase muscle mass and build muscle strength.

Each muscle in your body is enclosed in tough connective tissue known as fascia. Fascia holds your muscles in their proper places. This tissue can also restrict muscle growth. Even though your muscles want to grow, fascia is so tough that it can deny the muscle the room to expand. It's like trying to stuff a large pillow into a small pillow case. If the connective tissue around your muscles could not expand, the size of your muscles wouldn't increase, regardless of how hard you train or how well you eat. However, if you imagine yourself stretching the pillowcase and expanding it, you can create more room for the muscle to expand and fill that new space. By stretching your muscles under specific conditions, you can stretch the fascia and give the muscles more room to grow. The best time to stretch to expand the fascia is when your muscles are pumped full of blood. When muscles are fully pumped up, they are pressing against the fascia. By stretching hard at this time, you increase the pressure, which leads to expansion of the fascia and building muscle mass and strength.

Stretched Towards Change

Never allow yourself to languish in a state of immobility where you fail to grow. You must choose a direction and move forward. Your direction can be defined as a direct course of thought, action, or a motivating purpose. When you stretch to expand or move outside of your "comfort zone," you develop your abilities and grow. As you move forward, you will experience discomfort, but you cannot allow it to inhibit your growth.

During difficult times, God wants us to come to him. The Holy Spirit is our comforter. If you feel uncomfortable, disconnected, or alone, take a moment to be quiet and still, and you will feel a nudging from God. Allow God to direct you. As you pull closer to him, he will draw closer to you.

If you throw a frog into boiling water, it will jump out. However, if the same frog is placed in lukewarm water, it will remain in the pot. If you slowly increase the fire under the pot, the water will become hotter and hotter, but the frog will still remain there. The temperature changes so gradually that the frog doesn't even recognize the need or his ability to jump out. The water eventually boils, and unfortunately, by then it's too late - the frog has been cooked alive.

When the logs and rubble were in my backyard, I could have chosen to do something about it before the bugs began to breed. I could have given the lumber away or put it in the trash. Either choice required me to make a decision or do something about the problem. Failure to take action was not a neutral option. It was a choice that provided a breeding ground for maggots while I ignored that nagging feeling inside me telling me that I ought to do something about it. Not making a decision to resolve or eliminate a problem is the same as *agreeing* to allow the problem to become worse.

> **"A boat was meant to dock in the harbor, but it was not meant to remain there."**
> *- Author Unknown*

No one should allow themselves to remain stuck in their comfort zone for too long. When you have a problem or obstacle to overcome, remaining in your comfort zone is not always the safest or wisest option. In corporate America, workers who remain in their comfort zone rather than expanding their capabilities and diversifying in their retirement planning are more negatively impacted by downsizing or the loss of retirement investments. God's plan for your life requires you to continually seek opportunities to grow, plan ahead, and help others. The safest place is always walking in the will of God.

Many people have found the strength within to move beyond their circumstances and propel themselves into success despite their shortcomings. In life, you will encounter adversity. You'll have to deal with "naysayers" and setbacks that make you feel like giving up, but these are the times when you should trust God and allow him to help you increase your knowledge and develop new skills. Look for opportunities and resources that he will place within your reach. Search within for inner strength, wisdom, and resourcefulness while pursuing your passions and dreams.

You are in the driver's seat. Never expect other people to do for you what you should be doing for yourself. You can empower yourself by reminding yourself of your past successes and the successes of others who can provide inspiration and direction. Knowing how others were able to overcome adversity and achieve their goals successfully can help you during those times in life when you might feel hopeless. If others did it, so can you. Identify family and friends who can encourage you to fulfill your goals and support you, especially during difficult times.

Paul Orfalea, founder of Kinko's, the world's leading provider of business services, started his business in a 100-square-foot room with a $5,000 loan. As a young child, Paul suffered from severe dyslexia, but he looked beyond himself. He saw a need, an opportunity, and a big demand for printing on college campuses. So he pursued his vision on campuses where people were computer savvy and needed the services he could provide. There are now approximately 1,100 Kinko's centers worldwide. However, Paul's greatest happiness comes from helping families. With his financial success, he is now able to spend much of his time and resources as a philanthropist providing help for the learning disabled and single mothers. As you receive clarity in your purpose and vision, you will realize that your purpose is not just for your self-interest but to help others. There is nothing more fulfilling than contributing to a cause and need that is near and dear to your heart.

Life's Continual Rhythmic Motions

A few years ago, my mother suffered a massive heart attack. She required a triple bypass, and after the surgery she was attached to a heart monitor. I saw the monitor line go up and down continually. When my mother coughed, an alarm would sound off and the line on the monitor would show excessive activity and then eventually return to a normal rhythmic motion. The first few times this happened, I was very concerned, so I would run and call the nurse. The nurse explained that this was expected. My mother's heart was healing from surgery, and coughing was a part of the process. Her body was adjusting appropriately, and the heart monitor line was moving up and down consistently to confirm that. After she was released from the hospital she also had to follow the doctor's instructions for further recovery. I thank God that my mother is doing well and is healthier than ever, but it required changes on her part, some of which were painful.

Our life experiences reflect a continuous rhythmic motion, with some periods that are more sporadic than others. If you think back on your experiences, you will recall that they varied. When you recall a negative experience from five years ago or more, you can also recall how you made it through. You handled the situation, developed resilience, and it worked out - you're still here.

Humans are not meant to remain stagnant or live only in their comfort zone. When you get out of your comfort zone, you will be stretched and you may experience pain, but the end result will always be better than what you could ever otherwise achieve. You have no way of knowing if you can do it, until you try. **Your dreams are worth it.**

We often hear stories about people who have been successful. Why can't you be one of them? About 80 years ago, John R. Simplot ran away from home at 14 years of age because he was tired of milking cows. He then built a fortune growing potatoes, and his company now supplies McDonald's, Burger King, and other fast food companies with french fries. About 50 years ago, Bill Gates dropped out of Harvard University to run a small startup company called Microsoft. He is now the richest man in the world. These men were driven by an inner passion and provoked to achieve something beyond what may have appeared impossible.

It is important that you not remain comfortable accepting the way things are in your life. Change is not only an opportunity for growth, but it is also healthy and conducive to your development.

<u>Summary</u>

- Things we don't take care of can be a breeding ground for bad habits and chaos in our lives.
- As you move forward in life, anticipate some discomfort. It is through this discomfort that we have an opportunity to grow.
- Change is an opportunity for growth. It is healthy and conducive to your development.
- In life, you will encounter adversity, naysayers, and setbacks that can cause you to feel like giving up. These are the times when you can look for support outside of yourself and search within for solutions that are already there, waiting to be

recognized, so that you can continue to pursue your dreams and passions.

Application

1. On a sheet of paper, write a description of your "dream." It should be a specific goal that reflects your passion or vision of success in your life. It can be a career goal or any other specific long-term or lifelong objectives. Don't be afraid to dream big. What would you really like to do if you could accomplish anything you wanted? What would success look like?

2. On another sheet of paper list the pros and cons of pursuing and accomplishing your goal. Follow these steps:

   • Fold the sheet of paper in half vertically to create two columns.
   • At the top of the left side, write "positives," and on the right side, write "negatives."
   • Number the lines on each side 1-25.
   • In the left column, list the positives of accomplishing your dream. Include the rewards of having achieved your goal, how it would feel, who would benefit. Also include the benefits of going through the required steps and why your goal is achievable. What knowledge, traits, skills, and resources do you have or can you acquire?
   • Then in the right column, list the negatives of achieving your goal, including the obstacles that may hinder you and the negative things that may happen if you meet the goal.

3. Review the positives for accomplishing your goal and compare with the negatives. Do the positives outweigh the negatives? If so, then it's time to formulate an action plan and get started. Use your positives to overcome the negatives. What options are available to you? Ask for input from family and friends who might like the opportunity to contribute their ideas or assistance. For example, your goal might be to establish a

successful business, but you can't afford to pay for help to get started. Possible solutions might be to use volunteers from a local high school or to ask a trusted family member or friend to help. You can overcome any obstacle. You might not know how to begin, but you can learn by reading, talking to others who are successful in that area, or volunteering for them.

OBSTACLE #4:
Allowing Fear To Control Your Life

Whenever you challenge yourself to realize your dreams and accomplish your goals in life, you will probably experience some form of fear. Fear is a natural response that most people experience, and many don't overcome it because they don't know *how*.

Fear may manifest as procrastination or low self-esteem. It can be a feeling of unworthiness or a feeling that you don't deserve to have what you want or what others have. You may feel that you're just "not good enough" and that the successes that other people achieve could never happen to you. These are all forms of fear.

Every dream worth pursuing requires some level of risk-taking, which commonly produces fear. However, fear does not have to keep you from realizing your dreams. You can overcome it.

The key to overcoming fear is to "do it anyway." Acknowledge it, but don't dwell on it or let it control you. Be determined to press forward, looking beyond fear through completion of the process of achieving your goal. Look at fear with a positive attitude and as an opportunity to develop your abilities as you overcome obstacles on your way to success.

If a particular fear is blocking the path to your dreams, it may appear to be a much bigger obstacle than it really is. However, if you *believe* that you can take control and overcome it, you *will*. Then once you have moved past your fear, you can look back and realize how small an obstacle it really was.

The voices of fear can be the past and present voices of family, friends, and others whose low expectations you have internalized. The voice of fear tells lies, but once you believe it, the subconscious remembers and acts as if the lies were true. This is why it is so important to be aware of your thoughts and beliefs and how they can be influenced by what you hear, what you see, and the people you associate with. Studies show that most people's annual income is within $5,000 of the people they associate with.

Robert Kiyosaki is a "self-made millionaire" who spoke at a conference I attended a few years ago. He said one reason for his success was that he wasn't afraid of losing all his money because he knew what it took to *attain* wealth. He was willing to take risks with his money because he knew he could never lose his most valuable possession - the knowledge and ability to succeed. In other words, he knew *how to* fish, so he didn't worry about holding on to what he already had. In his early 20s, he made his first million and then lost everything, but he walked away knowing that it was possible for him to achieve. So he did it again and again, further increasing its wealth each time.

People fear "the unknown" or what they don't understand. The first step toward overcoming fear is to identify what you're really afraid of. This is part of the "confronting process." You must identify the fear so that you can understand it, confront it, and develop a strategy to overcome it. For example, you may feel fearful about taking a class in an unfamiliar subject or applying for a job in a new field. Any situation that may be unfamiliar or result in the potential loss of what is "normal" for you can bring about fear. Fear can be produced by anything that is perceived as a threat or loss, whether it's the loss of a person, place, or thing. Actual or perceived losses and other negative experiences of the past can create fear and affect your self-expectations and future decisions.

Have you ever had a passing thought or an experience that made your heart flutter, or a situation in which you couldn't explain why you reacted the way you did or why you were so afraid? It was probably because at that time, you didn't understand why you were afraid. Whether the basis for the fear was real or imaginary, the effects were still the same. You still experienced anxiety, felt immobilized, or retreated back to your comfort zone.

In *The Language of Feelings* by David Viscott, M.D., the author explains that whether one's fear is based on a threat that is real or imagined, it generally feels the same. Stressful times cause fear, and fear triggers the mind to seek safety. Fear alerts us to defend ourselves, but it can result in undesirable long-term consequences if not resolved. There is a time for defensive action and a time for survival mode, but we were not meant to operate in fear on a continuous basis.

When you identify, acknowledge, and address your fears, you become less fearful, even if you don't completely understand them. It is also helpful to identify the *source* of a fear. When, where, and why did it start? Many childhood experiences are carried over into adulthood in the form of suppressed feelings, including a generalized fearful mindset. As you identify when and how a fear originated, you can begin to understand it and resolve it at its root and therefore provide the breakthrough that unlocks the potential in various areas of your life.

All Signs and Symptoms Lead to the Root

A coworker of mine who is a handyman told me that when he was in high school, he used to work with his father, who was a contractor. He didn't choose that profession as an adult, but he now uses what he learned from his father to do that type of work around his own home. One day he came to work very frustrated and explained that for the past week during his vacation, he had been dealing with a problem with one of the walls in his living room. Mold had been developing on the wall repeatedly, and this had been an ongoing problem for several months. He had tried various paints and patching techniques, but he finally resorted to having to replace the wall.

Well, his problems didn't end there. Days after he painted the new wall, it still had not dried. Baffled, he asked a friend to assist him, and he went back under the house to look for the source of the problem. While under the house, he realized that a pipe that he had previously checked for leakage was badly corroded underneath and the leaking water had been traveling up through the wall, thus causing the mold. The damaged pipe was the source of the problem, and the damp wall and mold were just symptoms.

Like with the homeowner's wall, the source of your problem may not be visible initially, but when you identify and address the *source* of your fear, its related symptoms will also be removed. Sometimes, a professional may be recommended to assist you in identifying the source of the problem. A professional can help to accelerate the healing process so that you can continue on your path toward realizing your dream.

It is important to look beneath the surface of a problem to identify and address it successfully. I learned this in a situation that occurred at home in my own driveway. There were weeds growing between the cracks of the driveway, and although I had pulled them up several times, they reappeared within a matter of days. In some places, the new growth was even larger than what I had pulled out before. I finally realized that I had been breaking off the visible growth above the surface, but I hadn't gotten to the roots, which were hidden below the level of the cement. So I went to the local Home Depot store and purchased some weed killer. I used it to destroy the entire weed this time, including its root. The problem was finally solved. Likewise, your ongoing fears may also have to be eliminated at their roots.

In life, you will feed one of two animals - your fear or your faith. Fear is like a potentially brutal beast - it must be tamed while it is young. The longer you let it grow untamed, the harder it is to control and the deeper the root of the problem grows. If you feed your fear by giving in to it rather than taking authority over it, it will continue to grow and become an increasingly formidable opponent. Most problems that are not taken care of will become bigger problems. However, if you choose to feed your faith and rise above fear, you can keep your dreams alive.

To Fear or Not to Fear

When our fears are understood and controlled, they can be used for positive ends. They can motivate us to take action in the form of exercising the courage to "fight" rather than yielding to fear or a propensity toward "flight." The key is to understand the fear and find the courage to press forward in a competent manner to get the results you want. Your fear can become your winning edge.

When you're afraid, abilities that you didn't even know you had will come out. One day when I was younger, I was chased by a dog. As my fear heightened, I ran faster and faster, and my adrenaline increased, which helped me to run even faster. I was with a group of friends, and when we arrived at a safe place, we looked at each other and started laughing and saying, "Boy, I didn't know I was that fast!" Until we were placed in that situation, we didn't know we could run fast enough to get away from a vicious dog.

We have all heard stories of mothers picking up cars that had fallen on their babies, or firefighters risking their lives as they ran into burning buildings to save lives. You are what you practice, and what you practice is what you will do in a heated moment or when faced with a challenge. Firefighters practice hours upon hours for the moment when they will do something instinctive to save lives, even if they are afraid. The same also applies for police when their internalized training takes over during a crisis situation. I'm not telling you to run into a burning building or jump in front of a bullet. However, most successful people experience fear, but they don't allow fear to control them. They "do it afraid."

The thing you fear doing is often the most important thing you need to do. Your fears can cripple you in your ability to climb over obstacles on your journeys through life. It is important that you get to the root of your fears and resolve them at their source rather than feeding your fear by continuously conceding to it and allowing it to control your life. Many of your fears are rooted in past experiences and false beliefs that have very little to do with the reality of your current situation. When you identify and address your fears, you will be able to redirect your energy and make better decisions.

It is important that you take authority over your fears by speaking to them - speak the truth about your ability to overcome obstacles, pursue your dreams, and achieve your goals in confidence. Find a place where you can literally speak out loud to challenge your fears and proclaim your ability to achieve your goal. Don't anticipate and dwell on the worst possible scenario. Find the positive aspects of every situation, use your strengths, and work toward success based on actual facts rather than fears. If you feed your faith, you will starve your fear. You can replace your fear with faith and action and you will redirect your energy toward alignment with your faith.

When you are developing a plan to pursue a desired goal, identify the pros and cons on paper and determine how you can prevent or minimize obstacles and recover quickly if you stumble or fall. Talk to others or get a professional to help you address stumbling blocks. Whether your challenge is sickness, financial difficulties, or the loss of a job or family member, you can talk to someone who has experience and can assist you in the area in which you are struggling.

Fear has to be confronted and controlled. Acknowledge what you are feeling and surround yourself with support. Studies show that students who do very well in school tend to have friends who are also high achievers and have good study habits. Our lifestyles and beliefs are the result of seeds that have been sown by us and into us by others. Through the "law of attachment," what you associate with will attach itself to you, regardless of whether it is positive or negative. If you associate with and speak to others who have been successful in particular area, you will gain insight and the strength to move forward.

> **Obstacle Buster #4: Even though you may be afraid, do it anyway. Don't allow fear to control your life.**

Your Destiny Is Your Discovery

As a boy, James Earl Jones had a severe stuttering problem. He refused to talk and was a functional mute for about eight years. A high school teacher discovered Jones' gift for writing poetry and insisted that he recite a poem to the class each day. Today he is "the voice of" CNN, Bell Atlantic, and King Mufasa in *The Lion King*. Jones is also known to millions as the deep menacing voice of Darth Vader in *Star Wars*. The very thing he feared, he faced. The thing you've feared in life is the very thing you need to do in order to overcome it. To overcome something you have to be consistent. It requires commitment, and also work. In fact, the word "work" is stated approximately 564 times in the Bible. Many times people fail to realize there is always something they need to do in order to grow.

> **"Opportunity is missed by most people because it is dressed in overalls and looks like work." - Thomas Edison**

In James 2:17, it states that "faith, if it hath not works, is dead." It is not enough to have faith but still refuse to take action. Many people sabotage themselves because of a poor self-image. Self-image is the picture you have of yourself within. It has nothing to do with whether you look as if you have it together or you can fool others. "What you believe to be the truth is your reality," deep within. Having low self-esteem will weaken you and limit your success. People who don't have a good image of themselves tend to live a mediocre life. They may suffer from feelings of worthlessness, walk in fear, and never develop to their full potential. Procrastination, low self-esteem, uncertainty, and feelings of inadequacy are just a few of what I would call "cousins" of fear.

> *"If we do not have an enemy within, the enemy outside can do us no harm."*
> *- African Proverb*

The Thief of Time

The key to your success lies within you and your ability to walk in purpose without letting fear stop you. You can be your biggest friend or foe, your own cheerleader or sledgehammer, building or destroying your dreams.

Procrastination is the biggest thief of time and can be a roadblock to your success. Successful people are the "doers," and procrastinators may have the best intention to do it tomorrow, but somehow tomorrow never comes. Procrastination can be very destructive, but it is a habit that can be changed.

Procrastination is one of the many symptoms of fear. When I was a child, my mother would frequently awaken my sisters and me if we had not completed our chores. She would make us do it regardless of the time. She would also say, "Never put off until tomorrow what you can accomplish today." Her voice still echoes within me, and although at the time when she was waking us up she may have appeared to be cruel, we later realized that procrastination was a bad habit that would control us if we didn't control it.

People who fear success can prevent themselves from achieving their goals because they're afraid to even try. They believe that success is good, but they fear failure so much that they might rationalize their fear of pursuing their goals by saying that successful people are lonely, disliked, and either exploitative or exploited by others. This is not necessarily true, but these are the perceptions of someone who looks at the world through the eyes of their fear.

<u>Perspective Is Everything</u>

Everyone has a self-concept or perception of themselves. Your perspective is everything. What you perceive is what you believe to be true. Only you improve yourself and image when you change your perceptions.

Your self-concept is made up of three parts - perceived self, ideal self, and social self. The perceived self is how you see yourself, the ideal self is how you would like to view yourself, and the social self is how others view you. Those who are concerned more with what others think about them may hold themselves back from achieving their dreams.

Identifying what you are grateful for can become an unselfish way to strengthen your self-concept. As you identify the positive things in your life and listen to how you can help others, it places you in a position to view yourself as contributing to society. As you list all the things you are grateful for it immediately redirects your esteem from victim to victor, bringing about self-worth.

<u>Summary</u>

- Even though you may be afraid, do it anyway. The thing you fear is probably the very thing you need to do.
- Acknowledge that you have fear in your life and begin to address it. Things not taken care of will expand.
- Only you can improve yourself and your image, eventually bringing change to your perceptions.

<u>Application</u>

Every evening, write down five of your personal strengths and five things you are grateful for that day (such as accomplishments or other ways in which you have positively impacted or influenced someone else throughout the day). Complete this each night. In the morning, pray to God for his guidance and clarity in your life and review your lists from the previous day. This is a great exercise to do with a spouse or friend and a good way to develop more positive expectations and thinking patterns. It also focuses your attention on the abundance rather than the lack in your life.

OBSTACLE #5:
Allowing Your Past Experiences
To Determine Your Future

You cannot expect to go forward while looking behind you. We all have some experiences or regrets with decisions that we did or didn't make. We would love to change them, but we can't. We cannot change the past, but we definitely can learn from it. If you allow past mistakes to dictate your future, you can never fully embrace a life of "opportunity."

> *"Difficulties seldom defeat people; lack of faith in themselves usually does it."*
> **Becoming a Person of Influence by John C. Maxwell and Jim Dorman**

In the world of baseball, one of the oldest sports in the United States, someone with a batting average in the 300s is considered very good. This means that the person was able to hit the ball an average of 3 times out of 10 pitches. Even though they failed or "missed" 7 times out of 10 pitches, in the world of baseball you can fail 70 percent of the time and be still considered a good player.

Remember that even if you have failed at an attempted task, had a bad experience, or made a mistake, that does not make you a failure in life. Each experience is an opportunity for us to learn and grow.

Difficulties Are Not Defeat

Several years ago I had the opportunity to meet a young lady who shared her story with me. For purposes of this story I will refer to her as my friend Belinda. She suffered years of physical and verbal abuse and felt tremendous low self-esteem and a lack of self-worth. The hardest thing for Belinda was making a decision to change her situation and take the necessary action. Pregnant and with a young child, she eventually left her husband and returned to school to begin a new life. Belinda eventually obtained a PhD in psychology. Belinda has since remarried and is very happy with her new life. Because of her passion for families and her experience as a battered wife, she now helps others. She expresses desires to eventually open her own battered women's facility educating and empowering other women to pursue and embrace their visions.

Belinda's experience is a story that helps others and can reassure you that you too can overcome your obstacles. Even though she had past experiences that could have easily caused her to throw in the towel and quit, she didn't. She made a decision to focus on the possibilities of the future. Neither Belinda nor I would ever advocate divorce but in certain circumstances it is necessary; in Belinda's case it was to protect herself and her children

It is important that we do not allow our past or current situations to dictate our future or determine our life. Where you are is not where you need to remain. Everything is subject to change. You are in the driver's seat. You can accelerate forward, apply the brakes as needed, shift to reverse, or remain in neutral. However, keep in mind that a car that remains in neutral can be pushed in either direction from the outside or roll down a hill out of control; but the best way to move forward is to decide where you want to go and how to get there and then move forward with determination, work, action, and effort.

It's Never Too Late

In life we all have experiences or past shortcomings; however, it is during these times when we can use our energy to push us and empower us to go forward and not become a casualty of life. My mother-in-law, Aldene, is a great example of this. After 34 years of marriage, my father-in-law became tremendously ill and became bed-ridden and unable to care for himself. Because of her love and commitment, Aldene selflessly placed her life on hold and became Dad's 24-hour care provider for over 17 years. When he died, she missed him, but she knew that God still had plans for her life. She pursued her purpose and embraced her passion for singing, acting, and music. She now shares her story with other women and has begun to act in musical plays, bringing laughter, joy, and encouragement to others. When asked what she would tell others experiencing a "second wind" at 65 years old, she said, "Know God has a plan for you and you are *never* too old." God definitely makes no mistakes.

> **Obstacle Buster #5: Embrace life, looking ahead, not behind you.**

It's never too late to embrace the future. Life is a journey and you are in the driver's seat. Continually move forward without comparing yourself to others.

Summary

- You cannot expect to go forward while looking behind you.
- Do not allow your past or current situation to dictate your future or define your life.
- It's never too late to embrace the future

Application

1. Identify five people in your life who have overcome an obstacle and endured a difficulty. Interview them and find how they did it and how they felt before, during, and after.
2. Emulate the qualities that these people have which you would aspire to obtain or develop within yourself.

OBSTACLE # 6:
Trying To Do It Alone

There is a synergy that is developed from sharing your dreams, goals, and life with others. Unfortunately; the cemetery is not just overflowing with dead carcasses but is filled with unexplored dreams, ideas, and witty inventions. "If you never live to your full potential or utilize all the gifts you have been entrusted with, it not only a waste but catastrophic."

There are people who are literally waiting for you to start your journey, allowing them to begin and progress in theirs. Life is a teacher, and every good decision, bad decision, or none at all is not a failure but a buildings block to the structure to be created. Remember if you do nothing that is exactly what you will build NOTHING...

Have you ever heard of a corporation, organization, or person that became successful without people working for them or with them? When implementing a vision, a leader is only as strong as the team he is guiding. No man is an island. In fact, some fruit trees need to be planted near two or more similar trees in order for them to bear fruit.

Humans naturally grow and excel the most while associated with like-minded people. The support of your family and friends is worth more than a 1,000 words.

I was 21 years old when I decided that I wanted to become a police officer. In the eyes of my parents and others, I was still too young (and probably would never be old enough, if it were left up to them).

My father was shocked when I told him I had applied to the department, but it was a sweet and sour taste for him because secretly he had always wanted to become an officer but was too old when we immigrated to this country from England.

My mother, on the other hand, was supportive of my decision but hoped that this was a phase and I would change my mind. My mother, like many mothers, was afraid and concerned for my well-being but loved me enough to at least let me try.

I share with you my father's feeling because sometimes with either spoken or unspoken words your parents or guardian live their dreams through their children. We can go to a softball game or a children's beauty pageant to see evidence of that. Please don't misunderstand this: I have no regrets about my father's significant support, because helping me through this process was the next best thing to him doing this himself, and the bottom line is that I needed the support.

However, make sure that it is truly your dream and not your parents' unlived dreams that you are attempting to fulfill.

Obstacle Buster #6: No success can ever be achieved alone.

The Synergy of United Support

When I was accepted to the academy, my family was so excited. My father went with me to purchase supplies and uniforms required for the academy. The first few weeks of the academy were very challenging, and I was exhausted. We began running the second day, and even though I had gone through a pre-academy class, which was a class reserved for the top 10 female participants who scored highly on the oral interview, I soon realized that the running was still brutal.

My sisters, parents, and close friends soon realized that this goal would take a community effort. My father began to shine my shoes, a family friend purchased and set up a punching bag, and they assisted me in practicing my techniques. Everyone had a job, from packing my lunches to preparing meals for both myself and my study group.

They washed my uniforms and made sure there were military creases in my shirts, gassed and washed my car, and of course quizzed me for tests. Everyone encouraged me and listened to my struggles and pain.

At my academy graduation, my entire family attended and cried as they saw me receive my diploma; realistically, a part of them went up with me. In fact, my dates for the graduation party were my three sisters and my two closest friends.

My family had cried and laughed with me, so it was important to share with them that time also. You see I probably would not have accomplished this goal without the support of my family and friends.

Everything that could have distracted me from accomplishing my goal was delegated, and they freely did it, not looking for anything in return except my success.

Not everyone has a family like mine, but we can always develop an infrastructure of friends. But it does begin with you giving the very thing you need for yourself to others.

> *"Two are better than one, because they have a good return for their work; if one falls down, his friend can help him up."*
> *- Ecclesiastics 4:9-10 (NIV)*

Utilizing All Your Resources

In the book *God's Words of Life for Leaders* published by Zondervan Publishing House, the writer shares a story about a young boy who unsuccessfully struggled to pick up a large log as his father stood by and observed.

The boy became very exhausted and upset, so the father soon intervened and told him to use all his strength. The boy replied, "I am," and the father responded, "You have not asked me to help you yet."

Many times, as humans, people attempt to take on tasks in life that would be a lot easier with the help of others.

In *The Purpose Driven Life,* Rick Warren shares that while at the bedside of dying people never once did they ask him to bring their diplomas or show their awards. They asked to be surrounded by people; people they love and hold dear to their hearts. These people wanted to be surrounded by people. What people fail to realize until their time draws nigh is that it isn't the *things* but the *people* that matter.

As with the experiences of life being similar to building blocks, it is important to acknowledge that even the best bricks or building blocks never can become a sturdy structure without mortar. Never be fooled into believing that you can accomplish anything alone or in your own strength. God is a greater power with the greatest strength. He literally works through people for his people.

All good things that you receive in your life are a direct result of God enabling you and others to accomplish his will.

There are people whom you do not know and have not yet met who will become a part of your dream. As you identify your gifts you will realize that your gift and assignment is not for you but for the benefit of others.

Despite All Odds

An example of being empowered against all odds and helping others is Richard Branson, a successful entrepreneur and founder of 150 enterprises that carry the Virgin name such as Virgin Airlines, Virgin Mobile, and Virgin Cola. He has a personal wealth estimated at nearly $3 billion; he has followed that personal dream and made the most of it. He suffered from dyslexia and was also near-sighted, which not only continually embarrassed him but also caused him to have a difficult time in school.

Branson's ambition was not something identified by the local school districts or testing process and was clearly overlooked. His talents began to surface during his adolescent years just at the onset of student activism in the late 60s. Branson, frustrated by school rules and regulations, started his own newspaper in an effort to focus on the students and tie many schools together.

His newspaper was a commercial success with his schoolmates, and his business partner and he advertised to major corporations and had articles by ministers of Parliament, rock stars, and celebrities.

This vision had become reality with the help of Richard's mother, who had donated four pounds (less than eight U.S. dollars). The headmaster (principal) of Stowe, where Richard and his schoolmates and business partner were students, wrote, "Congratulations, Branson. I predict that you will either go to prison or become a millionaire."

Of course Richard's pursuit did not end there. With the abolishment of a retail price maintenance agreement by the British government, stores refused to discount any records (music albums). Once again Richard saw this as an *"opportunity"* to offer records cheaply by using mail order delivery.

The orders once again flooded in and were more profitable than magazine subscriptions.

Coincidently enough, *all* 150 companies of Richard's make money even though he claims to have had no prior expertise in any of their businesses.

In an interview with David Sheff of *Forbes* Richard remarks, "It all comes down to people; nothing else even comes close." He believes in this philosophy so much that he writes all 5,000 employees a chatty letter from his notebook as he invites them to invite problems, ideas, dreams. **Your past does not have to determine your future...**

> *"The end of a matter is better than its beginning" - Ecclesiastics 7:8 (NIV)*

Summary

- People attempt to take on tasks in life that would be a lot easier with the help of others.
- It is not things but people who matter.
- All good things that you receive in your life are a direct result of God enabling you and others to accomplish his will.
- Your past does not determine your future.

Application

1. Do you know someone you can reach out to and help? (Remember that no one should ever withhold something good from another person. It could be an encouraging word or helping financially. It does not have to be much. It is the thought, the heart behind it, and that motive with no strings attached. What you make happen for someone else will be done for you.)
2. This week reach out and assist someone else - you do not have to know them. Make it a weekly regime and part of your daily life.

OBSTACLE #7:
Taking Action

When traveling, the airline normally allows you to carry two pieces of baggage at approximately 70 lbs each depending on the carrier. If you go *over* the maximum weight or number of packages it will cost you; there will be an additional charge. As with extra baggage in your life it will also cost you - not only financially but also physically - to prolong and fail to address issues.

Earlier in my marriage when my husband and I went away for a few days I would carry three weeks' worth of clothing. I never wore all the clothes, and because my husband carried all the luggage (which was very heavy), he began to insist that for a few days I should be able to fit everything in a carry-on or garment bag.

I now travel so much lighter and wiser, utilizing all clothing I carry. I may carry one or two suits for special events, and the rest of my clothes can be interchanged. I also try to utilize the cleaners and laundry service at my destination if necessary. Traveling lighter has made our lives much easier and less stressful while minimizing the possibility of lost luggage.

Like the weight load of a plane, the less baggage or "issues" you have in your life the easier it will be to arrive at the destination.

"Preparation" Is the Key to Success

It is not unusual that prior to a race, runners will monitor what they eat. They will wear the lightest clothing possible, and some will even go as far as shaving their legs (a runner once told me that shaving his legs knocked seconds off his running time). Seconds to us may not seem like a lot, but seconds to a runner can determine whether they win or lose a race.

It is between deciding to *start* and taking action that prior to *accomplishing* their goal most people give up. It is in this "action stage" that most people abort their purpose and throw in the towel.

> *"A thousand miles begins with a single step." - Author Unknown*

Taking action and overcoming obstacles with each step is something my client and friend Sue can truly share about. As an adult, Sue immigrated to the states from Korea. Although Sue studied English in her country, speaking English in an English-speaking country was very intimidating.

I began working with Sue when she entered the masters program. She was a teacher's assistant in an elementary school that was 85 percent Korean. Sue was not only very intelligent but also beautiful. However, she believed that she was inadequate in her education and job, feeling that she was not good enough.

Although she had a passion to teach adults and saw herself teaching at a university, she refused to listen to her heart. *"How could someone with such a strong accent teach an adult in America? How would they understand? Will they laugh at me if I use the wrong words?"*

These were just a few thoughts that continually provoked her.

Sue like many had low self-esteem and a lack of self-worth. Eventually she decided to settle and succumb to the pressures of society. She decided that being a professor was too high a goal and attempted to go against her passions and tried to become an elementary school teacher instead. Now as I explained to Sue there is absolutely nothing wrong with being an elementary school teacher; the early stages of a child's life are vital. But it has to be a passion and dream.

Nevertheless Sue attempted to take the (CBEST), which is a certification to teach in California public school, but *failed* it eight times. Sue soon felt she was a failure. Once again, when you fail a test remember that failing a test does not mean you are a failure. It could mean this is not the season or time. Sue felt tremendous pressure, especially because her coworkers and friends were all teachers, so her inability to pass the English portion of the test was heart wrenching.

For Sue, overcoming these obstacles was a process and required her to accept not only her passions but also herself. Of course in her eyes she couldn't ever teach adults if she couldn't even pass the test to teach children. But everything you need to live your passion and dreams has already been deposited within you before you were born or will manifest at the time when necessary.

Sue soon applied to a PhD program and was accepted at the University of Illinois at Urbana-Champaign and received a job at the university teaching - you guessed it - undergraduates. She enjoys her job and life and stated that if there is something she could tell others who are challenged by adversities, it is to "follow your heart, especially if you know what it is or what you want. It is your responsibility to protect your dream and regardless of the obstacles hold onto it. You cannot live your life for others. Sometimes that means going against the grain. You have to see and accept yourself how you are and what you were born to be." Sue made a decision to change regardless of how uncomfortable it felt. Within each of us I believe there is a greatness waiting to escape.

Getting Up Is What Counts

Let's face it, as a child it was pretty instinctual to begin to hold onto the furniture or someone's hand and pull yourself up. In walking, most children went from pulling themselves up to taking a single step and sometimes then falling. When we fell we didn't lie there. In fact most of the time you probably didn't even cry. You got up and continued on your journey.

> **Falling down is never as important as getting up.**

If you have ever watched a young toddler you will realize that they walk, touch, and crawl because they *can*. They do this in an effort to get or go to something that caught their attention.

Nine out of ten times infants are encouraged by others to crawl or walk and even run until they are literally into everything including running from their parents. It is then that parents in protection begin to tell them "no" and "don't touch."

These words echo and travel with us through adulthood; some are good and some are bad. Your fears, "no's," "can't," or "won'ts" become seeds and core beliefs that can hinder your adult decisions. As they take root in your life it becomes a core belief, in other words your REALITY.

> **"What you accept is what you expect in life."**

The hardest thing is to believe in yourself and the discipline to follow through. In pursuing your dreams and taking action what you put in will come out. Many people pursue life in search of the "pot of gold" or money, but you can never confuse your purpose with money.

There are many executives and people in prestigious positions making over six figures annually yet who are empty and unfulfilled. As with everything else, money truly has a purpose, but it cannot make you feel complete within.

Many people are wealthy and very incomplete and unhappy. In life the vehicle is your choice, and it is to drive or be driven by someone or something.

Even as a child, there was greatness within you. Being unable to do something was not even considered until you were *taught* to second-guess yourself, focus on your weaknesses, or doubt your abilities. As a toddler you had an "I can do" attitude.

"Taking action" means taking the necessary steps to accomplish the desired results. Many people never complete this step because of procrastination or some other form of fear.

> *Obstacle Buster # 7: Doing what is necessary can never be based on your feelings.*

Time Is Your Most Valuable Asset

Paula Dwyer, author of *How to Catch Time Before It Catches You* in her monthly newsletter entitled "procrastination" explains: Successful people have a clear vision of what they want to achieve and the necessary steps required to get there. Their tasks are part of a larger picture, and they put off or eliminate doing any tasks that would interfere with their desired results. Studies reveal that those who do not accomplish much only do pleasant things and refuse to eat what she explains to be "frogs or salami." Frogs is described as when you develop a daily habit that may be unpleasant but is necessary. Salami, on the other hand, can be large and difficult to digest but when sliced becomes manageable.

As I explained in the previous chapter "the life you are currently living is the result of a series of choices *YOU* made." Whether eating frogs or salami, both are uncomfortable, but the action and follow through are required.

Your time is the most valuable asset you have. Whether rich or poor we all start out with one thing in common: **Time.** Each of us has been allotted 24 hours daily, which translates to 1,440 minutes. What we do with it becomes a choice. None of us can save time or recycle time by attempting to relive anything we may have wasted. Once it is gone it is absolutely gone, never to come back to that split second or moment of decision. Our best defense is to utilize time to its full potential, and if until now you have wasted it, then now is the opportune moment to begin to change.

> *In the South is an old man with a rowboat who ferries passengers across a mile-wide river for ten cents. When asked, "How many times a day do you do this," he replies, "As many times as I can, because the more I go, the more I get. And if I don't go, I don't get." Anonymous*

There is a purpose you came to earth. You were not a mistake.

There was a plan for you before your parents even came into existence.

Regardless of whether your parents were married or even if you were a planned pregnancy, everything you could ever possibly need has already been deposited inside of you.

Each of us has been given a certain amount of time. **Time is a currency of heaven**. It can never be bought or reimbursed. We have time periods to learn, live, laugh, cry, and die - a season for everything. We all have to account for what we did or didn't do. Use your time wisely to invest in yourself, your family, and others.

"How are you spending your time?" Take inventory and adjust accordingly.

As you continue the journey of life learn to look for the diamonds that lie in the rough. Your secrets of treasure are in darkness, and your dismal times can become your triumphs as you **overcome and conquer your OBSTACLES of life.**

Summary

- Extra baggage in your life will also cost you not only financially but also physically.
- The less baggage or "issues" you have in your life the easier it will be to arrive at the destination.
- It is in this "action stage" that most people abort their purpose and throw in the towel.
- Falling down is never as important as getting up.
- What you accept is what you expect in life.
- Even as a child, there was greatness within you.
- Taking action means taking the necessary steps to accomplish the desired results.

Application

Overcoming obstacles in your life is a continual process. Regardless of the circumstances, the "formula" to your success remains the same. I strongly encourage you to purchase our upcoming workbook, *Overcoming Obstacles - Applications Book*, and make it a part of your daily life. As you regularly evaluate your goals and progress, your life's journey will become more enjoyable and fulfilling not just for yourself but also for your family.

www.ingramcontent.com/pod-product-compliance
Lightning Source LLC
Chambersburg PA
CBHW031305280526
45784CB00004B/1993

* 9 781438 925202 *